THE YEAR OF THE FEMME

Winner of the Iowa Poetry Prize

THE YEAR OF THE FEMME

poems by

CASSIE DONISH

University of Iowa Press
IOWA CITY

University of Iowa Press, Iowa City 52242
Copyright © 2019 Cassie Donish
www.uipress.uiowa.edu
Printed in the United States of America

Text design by Judy Gilats

The University of Iowa Press is a member of Green Press Initiative and is
committed to preserving natural resources.

Printed on acid-free paper

Library of Congress Cataloging-in-Publication Data
Names: Donish, Cassie, 1982– author.
Title: The year of the femme / Cassie Donish.
Description: Iowa City : University of Iowa Press, 2019. | Series: Iowa poetry prize |
Identifiers: LCCN 2018040181 (print) | LCCN 2018044071 (ebook)
    | ISBN 978-1-60938-636-8 | ISBN 978-1-60938-635-1 (pbk. : acid-free paper)
Classification: LCC PS3604.O548 (ebook) | LCC PS3604.O548 A6 2019 (print)
    | DDC 811/.6—dc23
LC record available at https://lccn.loc.gov/2018040181

for my sisters

Genevieve, Robin, & Jennifer

& for Kelly

What would it mean for the subject to desire something other than its continued "social existence"? If such an existence cannot be undone without falling into some kind of death, can existence nevertheless be risked, death courted or pursued, in order to expose and open to transformation the hold of social power on the conditions of life's persistence?

JUDITH BUTLER

She had been a gloomy boy.

VIRGINIA WOOLF

CONTENTS

THE YEAR OF THE FEMME

PORTRAIT OF A WOMAN, MID-FALL

Today she decides to be a dancer
She lies in bed to an urgency of silence

A certain twirling motion feels engaging
The morning turns when her lover isn't here

If he ever moves out, she'll think about getting a dog
Being a woman means needing a little protection

She gets a little anxious when he travels
The dog will make her feel safer living alone

Some women she knows have lived alone for a long time
They've longed for love
She's had lots of love, too much of it disquieting
She's longed for solitude
Are all women miserable, she wonders

She'll be safer when she's a dancer
The leaves out the window are having a good time

In the mirror she sees her own shape
Which has housed a certain kind of want

It's not that she doesn't want love anymore
But from now on she'll stick to ideas

She needs a little protection
Ideas are flexible, which protects their shapes

They're moving, spacious, she can embody them
She can ignore them for a while and come back later
They're still there: perfect
They don't mind her involvement with others
Today she wears a men's jacket and goes out into the bright fall

She keeps her heartbreak secret but not really
People can see right through her can't they

It's important to have a little certainty
It's important to believe in calm rather than calamity

Even if you're calm you stay a little heartbroken
And the basin of your heart is appropriately full

Being miserable is the same as being happy
It seems she keeps slipping on a binary

Is there a way to slip out of a binary into a body
Something a little more comfortable
The leaves are especially yellow and she enjoys it
She finds her own enjoyment disconcerting
The shadows of the leaves know exactly where to go

She is selfish because she wants what she wants
She doesn't want to negotiate about where to live or how
There are already enough limits on that

She is selfish about her time
Every choice is already a negotiation (the leaves are turning)
From now on she will negotiate with the world

She is definitely not a good woman

As she gets older
She notices that women are miserable and happy
She notices that some men are empty and try to make women empty
She notices that she makes a lot of generalizations
That are not wholly untrue but also probably come from resentment
Is there a way to shed a thing called "socialization"
Is there a way to shed gender but admit to its effects
Anger for instance is a season that passes too quickly
And she feels only love again
That's her temperament, she thinks

Anger then resignation then love
It seems to her to be unproductive
Maybe she should alternate the order
Or there should be some other step, like action
Instead there are waves of feeling
She takes a walk and feels happy (the air is cold)
She doesn't change anything
She's really good at resignation
She's not very good at anger
Maybe this is why she doesn't change
She prides herself on her practice of acceptance
It's really resignation, which is feminine, and shameful

This seems to be the pattern
Going outside is part of the pattern too
Each day there are fewer leaves on the trees
Each day there are more leaves in the street
Time is a puzzle with interlocking parts
Interlocking parts are meant to be unlocked
Each bit of metal has its own form
Although people are similar to each other
Each person is having a distinct experience
She is wearing a necklace of amber
Amber is the color of the day
It is the color of being a woman
At night she removes it

People are singular and different from each other
A truth over its opposite is also true, but squared
Or is it that a great truth is its own opposite
Or that the opposite of a great truth is another great truth
It's time to be outside and make an attempt
The air is a crowd of transparent sequins
She can't get past lovers out of her mind
No, just one specific past lover
And then another

Outside, one sparrow is flying in lopsided circles
Around others she gets carried away with other ways of seeing
There's something to being left alone

The unfortunate thing is being stuck
It's unfortunate to see life as unfortunate
No matter how unfortunate it is it's better to see it as fortunate

In the park she watches the squirrels in the grass
They're energetic, they move toward each other, then away
She wonders if what a squirrel wants changes

She wonders when she'll start saying what she is
She's not sure what she is
There, at last, that is said

•

She knows what she wants
She wants to separate this cloud from that cloud
That way light can roll out from between the clouds
It can roll out and give some things sharper edges
And upon other things will fall shadows
The effect will be variegation, which is particularly appealing to her
Variegation is a distracting element and it's exciting
For instance if she holds up a piece of glass it will be transparent
It won't be colorless, she can see colors through it

To be folded very neatly into a little pillow of water
That sounds perfect
Today she's going to enjoy the fact that he's gone
She's not even going to think about him

Small and large pillows of water are pleasant things to imagine
For those who like to swim
He's not a very good swimmer
She's not going to think about him today

A little pillow of water is something to be neatly folded into
A day is self-contained and if it wants to see what's around it
It might seep out and look at yesterday and tomorrow and beyond
No, it can't do that

She sees too much everywhere, always looking behind, looking ahead
To see something different is to be neatly folded

However there are various temporal features to consider
A folding inward is a potentiality but one with a time limit
The way the ground rises to meet the bottom of a shoe
She's not going anywhere in particular
There is a way of attending to what the body is feeling
There is a way of seeing that could enact a different way of being
A different way of choosing where to be or who or how
She pauses in the center of a field
It doesn't matter how many days are like this, today still looks like this
She likes how it looks out today is an understatement
The colors of fall mean so much to a certain animal
She means the kind of animal she is, the human kind
The field looks like it's moving away from her

At the edge of a field a thought waits
Putting it this way gives agency to the thought
It's important to her that it can be said this way

At the edge of a field a feeling of arriving waits
Arrival is not a rival of departure
The two have to work together to make anything happen

All the clocks move together through time
In a flock of birds, some birds are a little behind
All the birds are held together by a principle of form

She watches all the clocks gesture at once
The clock in her kitchen
The clock in a past lover's living room

Somewhere, someone unplugs a toaster
Someone with silky hair looks up as she passes
There is an invitation in that glance

She sips whiskey from a glass
She thinks of the man on the porch
She often sees him there looking up from his phone
There is something delicate about him
Something soft in the expression
She wonders what he sees when he looks at her
Today there was a twitch between them
As if he were about to join her on her walk
Or ask her to come in
They would already know each other well
There would be little to say, just what came into their heads
She wants the fall leaves to stay
She wants them to because they won't
She knows this

What is it that she wants
Does she want a more assertive lover
Does she want to be a more assertive lover

Bark is peeling off the trees
The sound of it, if amplified, would spread
Through the veins of the air in the park

She wants to know how to do anything differently

The dead leaves lie huddled and still
They crunch under her shoes
As she exits the hotel
Hoping not to be seen as she is
Filled with absurd sensations, skin alive with wind
The leaves that are still on the trees
Are the bronze of his silky hair
The leaves on the ground are red
Everywhere she looks, the feeling of having looked before
The feeling of having waited to see
She doesn't put this feeling off anymore
She puts up with it, she gives in

The difference is always in the frame
She sees that now
When she closes her eyes the world does disappear
When she opens them she's interrupted, finds her body
As she left it, naked under the covers
She finds that thinking transports her to another place
Whose statement is not found
In solitude real arousal is still possible
The difference is always in the limits, given limits
Given a wet square of fall and an impenetrable week
Of surprising, passing obsessions

She wants a frame of tenderness
A tenderness is an over-ripeness
At the center of the frame is a single point
Which the senses travel toward moderately
Or aggressively depending on the air's density
In theory a given point is never reached
Becoming is always incomplete
She knows that if she steps forward, then forward again
Over and over she'll make it to the park
Where fall berries glow intensely in the cold air
She'll make it back home
Where the spines of books flicker on their shelves
Her nipples harden

Today the leaves crack like glass, they let the wind in
Today she has mixed feelings
About pronouns and also the snow
That began in the night and continued into the late morning
In which she sits near another, reaches for another's hand
A version of herself drinks coffee slowly
A pour of cream, a pour of whiskey
A ray of sunlight slips through a gap
The room swells, then shrinks
She pictures a different room, then stops
Starts again, then stops
She could start again

ONE FLUENT GREEN BLAZE

THROUGH A KEYHOLE, A VIEW

Back when I couldn't
               speak clearly

We placed the kettle here

On our mattress, to catch snow

The books grew desperate, we saw it

How they changed
                  their story

The song poised in the room

It wore your pink coat

    *

Birds chirping in the dark

Do they recognize

That bough that is a lifeboat

I imagine when birds dream

Their eyes reflect the flood

Look how mine became
                    emergency rooms, indoor

Swimming pools, an old building

Burning down in a neighborhood

I used to live in

          *

Yesterday I read all your books backwards

Starting at the root

Look how a melody paused
                    in the branches

Nestled there like the round
                              orange

Lanterns the politicians arranged
                         to trick the crowd

To please them

          *

You need your pills

You come to the kitchen

It's late, which is relative

In a vase on the table, you see only stems

I pour the water out

First
    on your fingers

Then moving up your arm toward where

Your voice bouquets
           at the sill

Here, I'll turn away

From the small orange bottles in my pockets

Toward the open window

DESIRE AND THE SOCIAL

Desire is personal, it is
private, woven into the home hours,
the hours of the body, waking
hours, sleeping hours, time
in the shower, getting dressed,
thinking of her, this lack
of sleep is personal, it is
private. Desire is singular,
individual, physical, it is
psychological, at the restaurant
her hair was in her eyes
and I wanted to push it aside.
Desire is social, it is the street,
the train, the business hours,
the ads that rush through our
bodies from the moment we can
see, beauty is in the eye of
society, lust is in the body
of society, the animal of me longs
for other animals of my kind,
this longing is shaped by phrasing,
by passages of books, by scenes
in films, the hair in the eyes,
a hand's subtle touch, desire's
in the clothes, the way we've seen
actors remove each other's
on camera, the man enters the library
and in a moment of revelation,

the woman realizes she loves
him back, the moment so
powerful that suddenly they're against
a wall of books, he's pushing her,
lifting her slightly, her foot leaves
her sandal, "I love you,"
she whispers, her dress of green
silk drawn up around her waist.
I don't know why I feel the need
to apologize for wanting
to push her down and press
my lips to her skin, this softness
is private, this circumstance
is society, a desire heightened
by context, by the sound of voices,
which are social, and public,
there is no way to leave
the public sphere, no way
to leave the privacy
of the body, she is behind the names
of streets, names of spices, names
of body parts, countries, lipstick colors,
family names, layers of appropriate
clothing, city air and city signs, traffic
and lights, the news, and much of history
is beyond us, much between us. Yet this desire
emerges not from her but from inside
me, inside this body, I
should stop using her name
and call it by my own.

TENDERNESS

To grow up with a father
Who does not want
To be in the world

To be told from a young age
By a father
That he has trouble

Being
(In the world) that he
Has trouble and to grow up

With a sister who
Has trouble being in the
And another sister who

And there was a second father
Who also
And as an adult she has

Trouble finding those
Who do not
Have trouble / She finds this

One beautiful / Later
Finds that he / Like her
Fathers and sisters

Does not want to be
Has trouble being
But the feeling

Of being with those who
Is so familiar her limbs
Go limp with trust

INSOMNIA

I'm thinking about the "mystery of thought." I'm not thinking about it in a complicated way. Just how we can't actually "see" or "hear" thoughts, and how if someone does "hear" what's supposed to stay inside their head, that puts them in a certain category.

*

There's a branch that keeps throwing itself into my hand. "Fine," I concede, "I'm paying attention." It draws a picture, a room in the middle of the desert where a woman places smooth stones on a man's back. The man is her friend, her love, her twin who is sick. She says, "The weight of a stone stays when the stone's removed. See: the rest of your body will lift." He opens his eyes.

*

If the gods were real, our relationship with them would be complicated by our inclination to name.

If the gods were real, they'd say things like, "Do not lock me into any matter, lest you lose me."

And we'd say things like, "Don't you see that's also how we find you."

And they'd say things like, "You're winsome, you lose some."

And we'd say things like, "If I hold you in my hand and turn you, you change to reflect the salt marsh, its glint."

*

Memory: I lie on my side on the driftwood, facing the horizon. It appears vertical. The sun pours pails of shimmering into the sea, which I mention. He's sitting nearby on a rock, back to the water. He doesn't hear me. He watches the distant grasses swirl.

*

When the gods were real, they probably said things like, "The power of specificity is not that it calms but that it has an effect; it can calm or agitate, compel or dispel, et cetera."

When the gods were real, we probably said things like, "What's with the constant veil," and probably reached to remove it. The reaching being what lasted.

*

Memory: over field of open water, open sky. We watch the last torn edges of light disappear in the west over the sea, and this porch is where we've stood, and there's a great flat mirror moving inward, the tide.

The sea a glimmering counter always changing to reflect its counterpart, the time of day: white, purple, silver-blue.

*

I'd say things to the gods like, "Once I wanted to carry such beliefs."

They'd say things like, "What good was it."

I'd say things like, "Good for a change. For thou and thy art hath moveth sucheth cetera."

*

If he dies before I die, I'll press a button that says "record" so I can bring him all the words that accumulate from the moment of his death to the moment of my death. That sounds satisfying. He'll need a collection of sounds, little blue rushes to listen to later. If I die first, I ask the same. This is the sound of rain of rain of rain

MEANWHILE, IN A GALAXY

You can't sleep, there are little apples
                              in your eyes

Go to the orchard

Constantly lit
                    in the middle

Of the city
              the city

Next to the lake
                    that will swallow

The city whole

We'll sit on a rotting bench

A burning field
                    covering our legs

No, it's a blanket

Textures are rough
                    in the psych unit

      *

You need raspberries

Pistachio ice cream

And startled animal drawings

You need boxes to put
                        things in

And boxes to take
                    things from

Hey you, what's wrong

With having feathers

Let's talk about what's wrong

With our categories

Hurry up, paint an androgynous bird

On my stomach

What's wrong

With being a bird
                        metaphysician

                *

When the sun has almost set

We rush outside
           and head toward the edge

Of the property

We want to see
           the light bounce

Sitting on a rotting bench

Watching the city sky grow dark

We have to sing now

Because each tooth
           is a sparkling gallery

On whose walls

Are projected scenes

From old musicals

    *

Daylight glinting off dimes in the grass

Daylight, and our teeth don't feel
           different yet

Daylight on top of the city, on top
                              of the lake

Daylight through a sieve of fingers

Mimics the skyscrapers

    *

Dusk, and dusk
                    of dusk

I'll go to the Ministry of Health

Dressed in a gown
                        of peripheries

You'll go as the violet-green swallow

A summer resident
                    in the salt marsh

I'll even (yes) I'll
                build you wings

THE YEAR BEFORE OR AFTER
A VULNERABLE LOOK

Say we were once twenty years old,
collapsing on the sidewalk in the middle of the night,
the sheet of the future flung over us,
dry oak leaves, lavender buds, dyed egg shells, tissue paper,
all of that falling on us.
In a distant city, your watery letters,
amethyst chess pieces, friends.
Those rooms don't exist, the dark liquor, that apartment,
a night on which I caught an odd
expression. This did happen. Somewhere in the years
of separation, of travel, years of silence, years
of flowers watered by lovers,
and say my feeling wasn't always exactly the same,
each year the sense of amber.
Say anything. Light glints off the facets
of faces. The air in the city was different.
Your face was a composite of various
flowers, some new, some old. Say memory is a colony
of various residues—the smell of oranges
in summer, a line of a song,
someone's hand on my ass in a room
in winter, the voices of my parents,
my fear of the news, a photo of apple roses
baked by a man who could be
my father. The wish for fathers, a clover-shaped
window, its chamber of clover-shaped light.

HEAT WAVES

Hanging onto the edge
Of the pool, a rounded blue
I must've heard the weeping sometimes
Of my older sisters
Somewhere in that
Environment where
I came into a
Personality

*

I approach the window of
Morning, of opinion, of terror, of
Prediction, pull around me a patchwork
Quilt of hours—cream, dark blue, and pale
Blue, mahogany, plush rose—
Dare ye dare ye
You won't survive this
You'll only be
A self so long
So long, farewell

*

Floating in an emptiness
The little specks
Had more and more and more
And more, and more
Of what we'll call "desire" for lack
Of other concepts
Or we might say "will"
Or simply "tendency"
Or "motion"

*

I could say
"Desire stylized itself
To the degree that we're now
Standing here rapt
Looking back on a reflective
Past, held up in our
Own bodies, which possess us"
But each sound I utter
I wish to retract, to prove
My inadequacy

*

My father's death splits
Out of bedrock cracks
Layering gold and blue dust
Over the polished plains
Turmeric, crushed indigo
Any new experience of grief
Still evokes a rocky coast I saw
That year, the blanket of pink ice-
Plant covering portions
Of the shore
Waves dissolving
To sandy white
A spray of sand and water
Against a wooden shed
And a metal bell

*

What exists, exists
Suddenly, but is transparent
Eventually "becoming"
Through the mediation of
The senses, which add
Opaqueness, shape—
And we speak of
The real
However
We can, with borrowed
Words, these gendered

Words and bodies and
Days we possess until
Like pressure that
Causes heat, we cause
Heat, like heat that causes
Pressure, we are cause

*

The speed at which one wants to enter
The diseased cells of a friend's body
And begin, unerringly
To change them
To "mute" them—
One might imagine
Walking through a lightning storm
Enclosed in a blue
Sphere the diameter
Of one's height
A living breathing organism—
How can one catch the fire (go)
How can one shift the fire (go)

*

As a child I did
Thought experiments
On the beginnings of human
Existence as
We tend to be
Familiar with it
How sounds became
Symbolic, "had
Meaning"
How then in order to
Interact, meaning combined
With meaning, combined
Through parts of speech—
The one who swims
In the river is named
For swimming
Swimming is named
For the one who swims
In the river
Swimming is what
The god of the river does
The swimmer is
The swimming is
The river is the
God now
Of the river
Of the swimming
Of the swimmer

*

The cars outside
Hiss by, hundreds of dimes
Fly out a car
Window and scatter
The sun glows through
Plum-colored leaves
Lights them up
The color of blood, astonishes—
My friend was raped
By her friend last night, events
Ripple through brick
Suffocate the silver
The maple leaves, the dust

*

"See" specifically implied
"That's not me"—a problem of
Vision and yet
Herein, something we
Called "thought"
Stepped across that
Line, contradicted it
Or rendered it violable
How can we
Face our unknowing
While also trying
To imagine another
Person's life, to imagine

That face I see
Could be my face
We could have each
Been otherwise

*

Open ocean that seems
To express a human feeling . . .
Sleepy on a train and
Overhearing in my head
How my life, lacking
Continuity, feels today, not terrible
But empty, though one may recollect
The green and orange stripes
Of birds of paradise
Potted plants by a pool—
I skim lines in order to
Remember—how language
Bears desire—I can't
Separate that Tangier shore
From a moment, years
Later, when I desired
You, another way
Of saying I wanted
To evoke something
Beautiful aloud
In your presence
To counter the world with
A world

*

If I traveled close
To the speed of light
Through the galaxy for
A year
When I returned
My twin would be
Quite old, near death
Or already dead—
So time is not
Objective, though
This doesn't explain
How no matter who
Or what you are, a person
Or a dog
Or a stone or a fleck
Of dust, "time" is still
"Passing" in your opinion
I mean from your
Perspective the matter
That makes you is
Aging, and when you feel
The nearness of
An object of
Desire, time may warp
As when a threat
Is near

*

These thoughts are not
Poetic, death is not
Answerable, in the bay
On the night
Of the 4th of July, a friend's
Boat capsized, the body
Not found, in my mind
He's everywhere that touches
This sea out the cabin
Window—that bay
This sea, the sound—
Six days later we're
Out on a similar
Boat in the strait
I start seeing the word
"Dead" in quotes when I
Hear it
His body still
Exists somewhere
Beneath the blue
Corruption, a storage
Of stars

*

When I was wearing
A mustard flower
Net, delicately placing
Dandelion puffs
In a sick friend's hair
In his mouth
Saying only beginnings
Of sentences like "it doesn't
Matter—" how you still
Seem a kind of
Respite, a changeless
Encounter clustered
Around a theme
A tableau, a gold and
Black motif, bees lying dead
Among crushed pollen
And gravel—

*

Ferry my body
To the other side
Fill my mouth
With paper coins, vernal
Spillage, my disposition
Of bunchgrass, flags
Cattails from a different
Year, these souvenirs—
The water looks hard, looks

Wrong, the bay flashes
Dry, then wet again
The corruptible skyway
The corruptible kiss
The corruptible sentiment
These reversals will be
Instructions, will be
Clarity in some
Other realm

*

Grass of green foam
No angle here
Definable, each loosened bow
Is a logic just undone, slant
Of light on hills, on branches
Of oak, and here
The valleys proliferate
Yarrow proliferates
And the white bloom
That appears before
The blackberries, and green-black
Twists of oak—when
Does the world begin
To glow brighter?
Flock of grass tufts
Little bulbs on
Brambles, a railroad rips

Through grass, a metal
Ringing grows more
Shrill, animals are dead
On the road, and I
Exchange my measured
Ways for passion, and I
Am in the middle
Of a life—

*

What precludes corruption
May occlude, also, variations
In light, what narrows
Danger narrows
Growth, possibility
My fear protects me
Yet could convince me
To forgo everything
For safety, yet pain
Is a symptom
Of being alive
Please remind me
Of this when I'm
Afraid, I want to reach
Out and touch that water
To settle or stir it
I want to slit
That water open, swim

To the ocean floor
Lie in the cold
Belly of the wave
Instead I'm still
Looking out the window
At rocks covered
With lichen, a survey
Monument, a heron
That's been standing
Still for hours
On the shoreline

A GALE

THE LEAF MASK

she saw real birds
as wind-up birds with intricate
machinery; their whistles, the metal

architecture of their wings—she saw
them perched atop the hospital,
where exhausted women brought

catatonic lovers. She thought,
*all buildings are wild, inviting people into
their mouths. One day they'll chew*

*the crowd to dust, spit out bones, watches,
doves.* The crosshatch of winter
branches: another production

of the eye machine. In that season
of patterns, all that mattered
was motion; once again, stillness

meant danger. A strong wind
blew, a leaf the size of her face
flew against her face,

covering it, and she did nothing
to remove it. Right where her
eyes were, the leaf was slit—

TENDENCY

One could live, therefore

As if following a sparrow down a
                                    road of light

Sturdy bluebells

I paused the recording
                    of the grass

Grew hungry enough
                    to eat what was offered

Or would I still be holding the pear

And read all your books backwards

As if there is no
                    direction

In which one should live

A SURFACE OF NEEDLES

                    passing the hospital—the world
was drenched, wet gold with sun.
Everywhere, hazards. Unprecedented

flooding. The air bristled with
noise. She was in love, but not *with*
anything, anyone, anymore;

my love has no object. A lie?
Perhaps all she'd wanted was desire's
sheen—its look of depth—

not desire itself, which disintegrated
the closer she looked, but its one
talent, the ability

to discern . . .
                    try again:
in the hospital windows she saw
herself, an ever-new assemblage—

desire flows toward and away
from a center I experience
as thought; I am a machine;

thoughts were structures
through which she became aware
of correspondences. Strands of her

hair were copper, conductive;
the veins in his swollen hands: delicate
veins of palmate leaves, organic, animate—

THE TOWER

The answer to the technician's riddle was the word
torque. Rotational force. You found yourself at the
bottom of the ocean, surrounded by the dispersed
light of stars. Pressure breach. The sound of a single
gasp. On the escalator, the inky stamps of leaves. A
season of lust has something in common with any
season. You touched me like you were recovering
a past. I twisted myself into the blue-green rope
that would save you, I threw myself down to you,
willed you to climb out. *Please recover.* Let's take
the elevator, fifteenth floor to ground level, walk
out of this building. Walk away from this story. I'm
haunted by the endings I imagine. How fear rends.
It won't happen that way, I repeat to myself over and
over. When time stops, each cell in my body will
unlock. Each contains the same image: a face. The
mouth gapes open, but there is no sound. Nothing
to defend.

A FLURRY OF RATIOS

          it started with risk. The moving trees
pursued their pattern as before;
wherever a leaf goes, it sees; she moved

through the arbor where the rain beat;
along the bleached deposits of winter,
where doctors disappeared

into irregular groves. She was
convinced her curiosity was merely
an approach. A choice, a style.

Of course I see the danger, the eventual
death: aching nipples, whistling
teeth, a tongue like a match—

I'm sure I'll stop before it gets to that.
She corralled each object in support
of the argument. Either everything

had led to this, or nothing
leads to anything. Her obsession
was with percentages: *what can be*

accounted for? Cafeteria tables and chairs,
cardamom cake in a glass case, silent
wind thrashing trees outside. Lives

tallied up days while she, behind
her mask, watched. Look at all of you!
I'm not afraid, as you are, to unclasp

the past. Yet the fake pearls
at her wrist reflected his absence
in their mint hue—

MODERN WEEDS

All humans are marvelous, themselves objects—

Move back and forth between them

Along crowded hallways, along
                               coasts

Brush hands
                lightly

Don't worry
          about silence

Continuous activity, all our fine blooms

Submerged, carried
                    away—

Nurses, clipboards, flowers

Reality drunk on the scent

     *

Like the asters, I bloom
                    irrationally

My arguments are late, my summers
                              unsound

I'll try something else—

Occupying the world in a way

That surprises, but also

Seems to come from opportunistic
                              displays

Of blue and pink horses

Stubborn naiveté

         *

Convenience, a terminal rose

Split open, is attractive, but proves

Nothing—I prefer you, fireweed:

Rose-purple, striking, apparently

Disturbed—but beauty—

None of its elements

           has any sense

The beautiful astronomy

Can stop

Nothing

     leaves me broken

Like the memory of you breaking

Your skin

         open

Yet to abandon the image—

Would I be blinded

         by such

    *

Somersault toward

The pale meadow

I mean, away

     from the ditch

Break from the musk mallow's

         prejudice—

Knowledge is intricate
confidence, dishes

Nested
on the lawn

Belief is the heart-shaped

Blade in the garden—

*

Presence is here

The point I want to make

Traverses the repetition
of the theme—

Your touch was
a healing tonic

But aggressive—I prefer

Shade and mint, eggs, warm oats

Blue vervain's
dense flowers

Force us to remember

The blue-violet tone in lovers' speech—

Movement that renews

     *

I have failed in extending

This flow, this cascade

A dog's coiled tongue, blueweed

Growing by the highway near
                    the turnoff

Bright yellow fiddlenecks, disturbed

I have lied, I have not

Been speaking, I have not

Been able, I have simply

Talked as if there were
                 a domain

One could relate to by some sort

Of referential gasp—

Impressive
buildings

Do you love me?

Largest hospital in the state

The campus stretches
a year

It is no use, the past—

Make me alive
again

*

I shouldn't be surprised

Short hours, all the objects
exact—

Styrofoam, coffee, electrodes, rent

Sky-blue teeth of chicory petals

Divinities in the
waiting room, pay attention

Perhaps be cured

Build a flock of wood
                    pigeons

                *

Nightingales and frogs, enter the ward

Yellow star-thistle, settle invisible disputes

Ivory skeleton, deal with internalized hate

Neither science nor religion is fitting

Love, attractive centaur, follow me now

Into Oregon, Washington, California

Say again: here, alive

Not to designate, but to speak

A FOLD IN THE ACT

standing at the frozen fountain's
edge, she recalled sitting down
at the table of laments

for a meal of ice
and ideas—how the mouth
of the man across from her

was an unsteady line, the lamplight
a whorl of pale weeds;
how suddenly she was outside

and couldn't re-enter the house:
a dollhouse. The two
figures inside—she saw

herself through frosted glass—
were static. The interior appeared
as a fallow field. A thing is always

doubled by also being
an example of itself, she thought.
Yet there are moments when objects—

his wristband lying
on the kitchen counter, the sharp
knives shining in the dresser drawer—

snap into being, are only
themselves, irrevocably,
unequivocally. In fact,

this happens regularly—
and it proves . . . and it proves . . .
she imagined a mirror pivoting back

and forth so that it reflected,
alternately, a figure,
and a reflection of the figure

in another mirror—

THE YEAR OF THE FEMME

Someone said a journey starts with voice. I grew up swimming in a slow-moving river, in words like sister and girls. I knew a waist was supposed to be soft, knew when it should be covered, when revealed. Now I move through terminals, other places move through me, other words. I follow a sign, I refuse to neaten the disorder. Each object is assigned a role, a gender. Eye shadow. Boxers. Musk. Bruise.

The pleasure he said / Finding one's way

In a new body / My star anise

My amber, powder / His eyes I painted

Touched his wrist / Felt a pulse

There / (I felt her pulse

Your heart is beating, yes, despite your scars. Here is a recorded scent. *Tell me*, we say to each other. Say there will be sunlight. In public I wear lipstick the color of rust. I tell you about my sexual fantasies. How I'm a man in them. How it's been this way for as long as I remember. Your body is wrapped in ribbons of water. I remove my tie. I could cover your body with mine. I could make it warm. Don't go under.

Passing windows / Am I in that frame

Your first skirt / Blossoming

A name's transparence / Fluorescent lights

The ringing knocks / The wind out of me

Could I breathe where / (A carved ankle

You place objects in front of me on a table, tell me
to pick them up, to hold them as long as I want: a
piece of driftwood, sand dollars, these objects from
the sea. In an election year, I give you a scarf, a light
bulb, broadsides. We want to ignore flags. We make
each other's bodies blush with blood. After, I watch
you put on leggings. The heat picks up—

Mosaic of memory / Electrodes

Uneven path leads / To a creek

Electric current / A past clean enough

It might be *winter again* / No: it's spring

Summer / (You have no memory of

I want to describe a place that doesn't exist (anymore).
Time passes, but this could change. Blue cabin at
the water's edge: clouded windows, chipped paint,
a musty smell. We leave the doors open while we
sleep on a mattress, after. My eyes open, I see your
long body, after. We sit on wooden stairs grown
through with island grass, after. To be oneself with
another—

Though not children / The first time

We straddle / How names happen

In the world I / Wake in the loft

Bright irises / Brutal light

There / (Your thighs

A warm day in May waits on the other side of the sun. It's several years earlier. Some buildings haven't been built. I think you were a woman even then, but the face was blurred. Someone spoke with your mouth. Someone spoke with my mouth. The word *spectrum* becomes an obtuse angle, temporal. You say your voice is deeper than how you imagine it. Lately, if mine is recorded, no sound plays back.

The café / The balcony upstairs

Could see past / The monkey puzzle tree

Its green fish bones / Waxy scales

We the thick / Buds in the park

The far mountains / (The past

I hear your old name. I promise to drown it out.
There's a building we pass through, the color of
sand against a spring sky. I see that night, a highway
underpass, our walk through the old finishing
school. We followed the sound of a piano. We
stopped at the edge of the stairs, where a high beam
shone down into an empty room. I pulled (the heat
lifted) my shirt up—

If you kept playing / I'd listen

All year / You turned to me

Please, you said / I like it

Sometimes I am / Something else

You turned to me / (Touching

I look through photographs: cattails, your arousal at different times of day, a red poppy, obscenely large. I imagine you're the one whose hand dangles from the hammock. The textures are soft: colors not well preserved, as though kissed off. What isn't in the photographs is motion, your hips when you walk. The images bring back sensations, my arm around your waist, the smell of the salt marsh, the sound of the summer flocks—

Abstract to form / Your profile

Orange fish jumping / Out of the sun

We eat ice cream / Throw our cones

This rock is mine / This room is ours

And later, a click / (The shutter

I'm in a neighborhood of mirrors, adolescent
flowers, and the sound of footsteps. The question is
how to travel, to cross to you. Traverse. Objects glow
in real and unreal places, daylight and remembrance.
I see a threshold in the distance, but what if you
don't make it that far? I lived in fear. In letters, wrote
sentences about you like, *they don't seem like themself*—

Sea green garment / Still wet on the stair

This flower, we said / Breathe anywhere

And bees / Get tired, go home

To their cells / No: to pastel boxes

Stacked in the field / (A stacked heel

The world we tried to leave, we were still in it. If we turned the radio off, we still heard it. I hope now that I was wrong. That I can be good. That I won't drown with the weight of trying. The act of caring. We both reach for the mascara. It washes away with saliva. To nurture, to destroy, to submit, to master: we take turns. Is this a kind of answer—

(You are) this house I / Keep circling

Exterior / A permeable blue

I tried to enter / To say again

The conditions for love / Seem to be

And agency / (In spite of

High above the river, a silver vineyard. I'm walking
down a row of empty vines. I try to recall my shape,
my own weight. Cold slashes, this place of pronouns,
tinsel. In another time, unflinching, I swam to catch
each floating note, I sang. The river then was warm,
the green of broken bottles. If I speak now, I might
sometime sing again—

In spring the heavy / Smell of sheets

The smooth shine / Of the lilac-covered

River: *there* / No: rope in the river

Cellophane flower / Salt water taffy, the past

In wax paper, take this / Flowing and me

ACKNOWLEDGMENTS

In "Portrait of a Woman, Mid-Fall," the line "The dead leaves lie huddled and still" is from Robert Frost; ". . . another place / Whose statement is not found" is from Emily Dickinson. "One Fluent Green Blaze" is a phrase from Virginia Woolf's *The Waves*. "A Flurry of Ratios" includes moments that are indebted to T. S. Eliot's *Four Quartets*. "Modern Weeds" appropriates some of its language from Bruno Latour's *On the Modern Cult of the Factish Gods* and Ronald J. Taylor's *Northwest Weeds*.

Grateful acknowledgments to the editors of the following journals, in which versions of these poems first appeared, sometimes under different titles: BOAAT, "Desire and the Social"; the *Cincinnati Review*, "Through a Keyhole, a View"; *Forklift, Ohio*, "Insomnia" and "The Year Before or After a Vulnerable Look"; the *Iowa Review*, "The Leaf Mask"; *jubilat*, "Tendency"; *Sixth Finch*, "Tenderness"; *Trigger*, "Meanwhile, in a Galaxy"; *Tupelo Quarterly*, "A Surface of Needles"; and TYPO, "Modern Weeds."

Eternal thanks to Brenda Shaughnessy, and many thanks to Cole Swensen. Much gratitude to Jim McCoy, Meredith Stabel, Gemma de Choisy, and everyone else at the University of Iowa Press for bringing this book to life.

I'm indebted to Mary Jo Bang and Carl Phillips for their brilliance, generosity, and wisdom as mentors. Immense thanks to Stephanie Dering, Niel Rosenthalis, James Scales, and Paige Webb, as well as the other writers who were in workshops with me at Washington University in St. Louis. Special thanks also to Dan Beachy-Quick, Timothy Donnelly, Saskia Hamilton, francine j. harris, Rick Kenney, and Claudia Rankine. And thank you to Nancy Pope, the Olin Fellowship, and the English Department at WashU for generous support.

Thanks to wondrous friends Laura Bylenok, Melissa Dickey, Zach Savich, Andy Stallings, and Jay Aquinas Thompson. Thank you to everyone in my family, especially Sheila Munsey, Genevieve Munsey, Robin Munsey, Jennifer Donish, Lorraine Munsey, Lauren and Jamie Stephens, and Greg Heet, for ongoing support and encouragement. And thank you to Kelly Caldwell, whose presence in my life transformed these poems.

Iowa Poetry Prize
and Edwin Ford Piper Poetry Award Winners

1987
Elton Glaser, *Tropical Depressions*
Michael Pettit, *Cardinal Points*

1988
Bill Knott, *Outremer*
Mary Ruefle, *The Adamant*

1989
Conrad Hilberry, *Sorting the Smoke*
Terese Svoboda, *Laughing Africa*

1990
Philip Dacey, *Night Shift at the Crucifix Factory*
Lynda Hull, *Star Ledger*

1991
Greg Pape, *Sunflower Facing the Sun*
Walter Pavlich, *Running near the End of the World*

1992
Lola Haskins, *Hunger*
Katherine Soniat, *A Shared Life*

1993
Tom Andrews, *The Hemophiliac's Motorcycle*
Michael Heffernan, *Love's Answer*
John Wood, *In Primary Light*

1994
James McKean, *Tree of Heaven*
Bin Ramke, *Massacre of the Innocents*
Ed Roberson, *Voices Cast Out to Talk Us In*

1995
Ralph Burns, *Swamp Candles*
Maureen Seaton, *Furious Cooking*

1996
Pamela Alexander, *Inland*
Gary Gildner, *The Bunker in the Parsley Fields*
John Wood, *The Gates of the Elect Kingdom*

1997
Brendan Galvin, *Hotel Malabar*
Leslie Ullman, *Slow Work through Sand*

1998
Kathleen Peirce, *The Oval Hour*
Bin Ramke, *Wake*
Cole Swensen, *Try*

1999
Larissa Szporluk, *Isolato*
Liz Waldner, *A Point Is That Which Has No Part*

2000
Mary Leader, *The Penultimate Suitor*

2001
Joanna Goodman, Trace of One
Karen Volkman, Spar

2002
Lesle Lewis, Small Boat
Peter Jay Shippy, Thieves' Latin

2003
Michele Glazer, Aggregate of
    Disturbances
Dainis Hazners, (some of) The
    Adventures of Carlyle, My Imaginary
    Friend

2004
Megan Johnson, The Waiting
Susan Wheeler, Ledger

2005
Emily Rosko, Raw Goods Inventory
Joshua Marie Wilkinson, Lug Your
    Careless Body out of the Careful Dusk

2006
Elizabeth Hughey, Sunday Houses
    the Sunday House
Sarah Vap, American Spikenard

2008
Andrew Michael Roberts, something
    has to happen next
Zach Savich, Full Catastrophe Living

2009
Samuel Amadon, Like a Sea
Molly Brodak, A Little Middle
    of the Night

2010
Julie Hanson, Unbeknownst
L. S. Klatt, Cloud of Ink

2011
Joseph Campana, Natural Selections
Kerri Webster, Grand & Arsenal

2012
Stephanie Pippin, The Messenger

2013
Eric Linsker, La Far
Alexandria Peary, Control Bird
    Alt Delete

2014
JoEllen Kwiatek, [Study for Necessity]

2015
John Blair, Playful Song Called
    Beautiful
Lindsay Tigue, System of Ghosts

2016
Adam Giannelli, Tremulous Hinge
Timothy Daniel Welch, Odd Bloom
    Seen from Space

2017
Alicia Mountain, High Ground
    Coward
Lisa Wells, The Fix

2018
Cassie Donish, The Year of the Femme
Rob Schlegel, In the Tree Where the
    Double Sex Sleeps